Light and Dark

Julie Murray

Abdo Kids Junior
is an Imprint of Abdo Kids
abdobooks.com

Abdo
OPPOSITES
Kids

abdobooks.com

Published by Abdo Kids, a division of ABDO, P.O. Box 398166, Minneapolis, Minnesota 55439.
Copyright © 2019 by Abdo Consulting Group, Inc. International copyrights reserved in all countries.
No part of this book may be reproduced in any form without written permission from the publisher.
Abdo Kids Junior™ is a trademark and logo of Abdo Kids.

Printed in the United States of America, North Mankato, Minnesota.

102018

012019

 THIS BOOK CONTAINS
RECYCLED MATERIALS

Photo Credits: iStock, Shutterstock

Production Contributors: Teddy Borth, Jennie Forsberg, Grace Hansen

Design Contributors: Christina Doffing, Candice Keimig, Dorothy Toth

Library of Congress Control Number: 2018945732
Publisher's Cataloging-in-Publication Data

Names: Murray, Julie, author.

Title: Light and dark / by Julie Murray.

Description: Minneapolis, Minnesota : Abdo Kids, 2019 | Series: Opposites |
    Includes glossary, index and online resources (page 24).

Identifiers: ISBN 9781532181818 (lib. bdg.) | ISBN 9781532182792 (ebook) |
    ISBN 9781532183287 (Read-to-me ebook)

Subjects: LCSH: Synonyms and antonyms--Juvenile literature. | Polarity--Juvenile literature. |
    Light and darkness--Juvenile literature. | Brightness perception—Juvenile literature.

Classification: DDC 428.1--dc23

Table of Contents

Light and Dark

Daytime is light.

The sun is **shining**.

Nighttime is dark. The car turns on its **headlights**.

The color yellow is light.

Bella wears a yellow shirt.

The color navy is dark.

Hugo wears a navy hat.

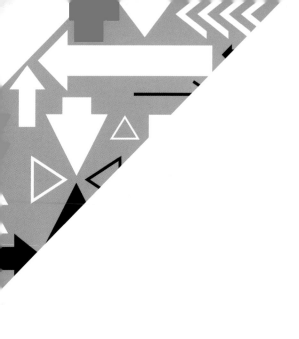

Andy has light hair.

He reads a book.

Jenny has dark hair.

She plays soccer.

Ellen turns on a light.

She reads a story to her bear.

Diego turns off the light.
The room is dark. He can
see the stars.

Look around you. What do you see that is light? What do you see that is dark?

More Things Light and Dark

canary

nickel

highlighter

bat

penny

pen and ink

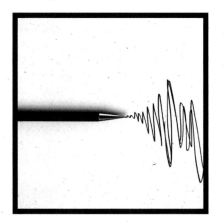

Glossary

headlight
a bright light on the front of a vehicle.

shining
to give off or reflect light.

Index

Abdo Kids ONLINE
FREE! ONLINE MULTIMEDIA RESOURCES

Visit **abdokids.com** and use this code to access crafts, games, videos, and more!

Abdo Kids Code:
OLK1818